Contents

Words that appear in the text in bold, **like this**, are explained in the glossary.

Iraq before Saddam

The Arab world, of which Iraq forms a small but historically important part, includes North Africa and the western half of that area between the Mediterranean and the Indian subcontinent which Europeans have traditionally called the Middle East. The Arabs themselves, a people with origins in the Arabian peninsula, spread out to occupy and colonize this wide area in the great conquests of the 7th and 8th centuries which followed the birth of the religion of **Islam**.

During the 18th and 19th centuries much of the Arab world fell within the borders of the Turkish Ottoman Empire, and when that empire joined in World War I on the German side many of its Arab subjects seized the chance to fight for their independence. The British and French welcomed Arab support against the Turks, but were unwilling to allow their new Arab friends any real independence once the war was over. Some states were given what looked like independence, but British and French troops remained on hand, ready to take action if their countries' interests were threatened.

British troops in Turkish Mesopotamia during World War I. After the war Mesopotamia became part of the new state of Iraq.

Iraq

Iraq was one such state. It was formed of three old Turkish provinces – Mosul, Basra and Baghdad. Borders were set by colonizing powers with little regard to natural or ethnic boundaries. Mosul was included, at least in part, because the British wanted control of its oil wealth. The resulting Iraqi population – 3 million in 1920, 24 million in 2000 – was 75 per cent Arab and 18 per cent **Kurd**. In religious terms, 95 per cent of Iraqis were **Muslims**. Of these, 60 per cent were **Shi'a Muslims**, most of whom lived in the south of the country. The other 40 per cent, which included all the Kurds, were **Sunni Muslims**. This meant that the Iraqi population was, and is, made up of three basic groups – the Kurdish Sunnis in the north, the Arab Sunnis in the centre and the Arab Shi'as in the south.

Sunnis and Shi'as

The division of Muslims into Sunnis and Shi'as happened in the late 7th century. It followed a dispute over how their leader (or Caliph) should be chosen. One group believed that the leader should come from the Prophet Muhammad's family, which was then represented by the descendants of his son-in-law Ali. This group became the Shi'at Ali (party of Ali), and are now known as Shi'as. The other group thought the leader should be the man with the most natural power. They took the name 'Sunni', which means authority.

Sunni Muslims make up the majority of the population in Baghdad, and in Iraq they have been more **secular** and tend to hold more positions of power. Many Shi'a Muslims, in southern Iraq, were largely excluded from Saddam's government and maintain a more traditional lifestyle.

The Turks had given the best administrative jobs to Arab Sunnis, and the British continued this policy when they took command of Iraq in 1918. They chose their wartime ally Faisal, a Sunni Muslim from the Hejaz region of Arabia, as the new country's king, even though he had never set foot in it before. They encouraged the creation of a political **elite** among the richer Sunni Muslims. Iraq was granted independence in 1932, but everyone knew the British were still in control. For example, when Iraqis voiced their support for Germany during World War II, they were quickly imprisoned.

After the war, the British tried to make their continued presence less obvious, and let the Iraqi government take most of the political decisions. Although the Sunni Arab elite was happy,

The Arab-Israeli dispute

After World War II, Britain effectively promised the old Turkish province of Palestine to both the Arabs and the Jews. This created a major problem, which Britain eventually passed on to the **United Nations (UN)**, and in 1947 it was decided to partition Palestine between the two communities. This was rejected by the Arabs, and **civil war** broke out between them and the Jews. In May 1948 the Jews declared an independent state of Israel in an area larger than that proposed by the UN partition plan. Five Arab states – Egypt, Lebanon, Syria, Jordan (then called Transjordan) and Iraq – then sent forces to help the Arabs, but the Israelis were victorious. The remaining areas of the old Palestine were taken over by Egypt (the Gaza Strip) and Transjordan (the West Bank and East Jerusalem).

The Arabs saw this defeat, and the establishment of Israel which followed it, as evidence of their own weakness and lack of unity. Twice, in 1967 and 1973, they went to war to reverse the situation, and on each occasion suffered another crippling defeat. After its victory in 1967 Israel occupied both the Gaza Strip and West Bank. The return of these territories, and the creation of an independent Palestinian state within their borders, eventually became the stated goal of the wider Arab world. Arab leaders who have actively pursued this goal by confronting Israel have usually been considered heroes by the Arab peoples. The USA has made itself deeply unpopular with most Arabs by offering Israel consistent economic, diplomatic and military support.

most Iraqis were not. Like many others around the world, they wanted an end to **colonialism**, and grew increasingly angered by their government's acceptance of a continued British presence. The Iraqi Army's dismal performance in the 1948 Arab-Israeli war emphasized how ineffective that government was, and riots at home lasted several weeks.

Arab nationalism

In the Arab World the struggle against colonialism was accompanied by a desire to unite the Arab peoples under one flag. A single Arab nation, it was argued, would be a powerful force in the world. **Arab nationalism** – not just Iraqi nationalism – was the answer.

Rebel troops outside the royal palace in Baghdad after the 1958 coup, which overthrew the monarchy.

The first to act on this idea were the Free Officers in Egypt, a group of army officers who overthrew the pro-Western Egyptian monarchy in 1952. Their leader, Gamal Abdel Nasser, became a hero throughout the Arab world for his strident opposition to the continuing Western presence in the Middle East. But his was not the only such influence. In the 1940s another Arab nationalist movement, the **Ba'ath**, had been formed in Syria, and through the 1950s and 1960s its influence spread throughout the Middle East. Like Nasser, the Ba'ath combined calls for Arab unity with demands for development and modernization.

Both the Egyptian Free Officers and the Ba'ath found followers in Iraq, particularly among the army. In July 1958 Iraqi Free Officers overthrew the **monarchy** in a particularly bloody **coup**. The King, Crown Prince and many of the old elite were killed, the rest imprisoned or driven into **exile**. A **republic** was declared.

Kassem

The two officers who had led the coup – Brigadier Abdel Karim Kassem and Colonel Abdel Salam Aref – soon fell out. Aref was an Arab nationalist who believed that Iraq should join with Syria and Egypt in their recently-announced (and subsequently short-lived) United Arab Republic. Kassem was an Iraqi nationalist who believed in sorting out Iraq first. With the help of the Iraqi **communists** and the Kurdish parties, he succeeded in establishing a **military dictatorship**. Aref, his Arab nationalist allies and the Ba'ath were excluded from power.

They fought back. In Baghdad and other Iraqi cities there was frequent street-fighting, and in March 1959 there was a full-scale revolt in the northern city of Mosul. Kassem survived this, but over the next few years his support slowly dwindled away. Ba'ath supporters criticized his failure to get a bigger share of Iraq's oil earnings from the British companies which controlled it, and his failure to foster Arab unity. In 1963 disgruntled Ba'athist Army officers and civilians overthrew the regime, and Kassem himself was executed.

Abdel Salam Aref (left) and Abdel Karim Kassem, shortly after leading the coup in July 1958.

Aref

A Ba'athist named Ahmad Hassan al-Bakr led the coup in 1963, but Kassem's old deputy Aref, who had been brought in to serve as a figurehead president, managed to establish a military dictatorship much like Kassem's. Ba'ath supporters, finding themselves out of power once more, went underground. In September 1964 they tried to seize power through another coup, but failed. Al-Bakr and his deputy, a young man from Tikrit named Saddam Hussein, were sent to prison.

Plainclothes National Guardsmen patrol the streets after the coup which overthrew Kassem in 1963.

But neither Aref nor his brother – who succeeded him in 1966 – showed himself capable of solving the country's pressing problems. In the north, Kurds seeking independence from Iraq were fighting government troops in a war which had already cost 50,000 civilian lives. In the south, the Shi'a Muslims increasingly resented their second-class status. The regime's failure to promote Arab nationalism annoyed Ba'ath supporters, and its oil deals with France and the Soviet Union annoyed the USA. In July 1968 the Ba'ath mounted another coup.

This time al-Bakr took the presidency himself. The seats nearest to his at the government table were occupied by the high-ranking officers who had made the coup possible, but further down the table, mostly ignored by the officers, sat the new Deputy Secretary General of the Ba'ath Party, 31-year-old Saddam Hussein. Within weeks his would be the only voice that really mattered.

Biography – The young Saddam Hussein

Saddam Hussein was born, probably in 1937, just outside the Tigris river town of Tikrit, some 100 kilometres (60 miles) north of Baghdad. His father, for reasons that remain unknown, had already disappeared by the time of his birth, and his mother soon married again. Saddam's Sunni Muslim family were poor and remained so, living in a mud brick house which they shared with a few animals. Saddam soon had three younger half-brothers whom their father considered to be more important than him, and he was probably glad to leave home at the age of ten to live with his mother's brother, Khairallah Tulfah. Khairallah was then a schoolteacher in a nearby village, but only a few years earlier the British had thrown him out of the Iraqi Army for joining a rebellion against them during World War II.

In the early 1950s Khairallah moved his family to Baghdad, and Saddam, now in his early teens, took a series of jobs, rounding up passengers for taxis, selling cigarettes and waiting at tables in coffee houses. Khairallah was active in politics, and one frequent visitor to the house was Ahmad Hassan al-Bakr, who would lead the military coups of 1963 and 1968.

Saddam Hussein in his thirties.

The rise to power

After allying himself with the Ba'ath Party, Saddam Hussein had risen to a position of real power relatively quickly. When Kassem and Aref first took power in Baghdad in July 1958, Saddam was only 21 years old. In the virtual civil war which followed he commanded a street gang of pro-Ba'ath thugs. In October of the following year, during a failed assassination attempt against Kassem, Saddam was wounded and forced to flee across the desert to Syria. He went to Damascus, where he finally joined the Ba'ath Party, and then on to Cairo. When Kassem was overthrown in 1963 he rushed back to Baghdad. Thanks to al-Bakr's influence, he was made a member of the leadership council, and more or less given a free hand. Saddam Hussein organized punishment units and visited the camps where Kassem's surviving supporters were held. There are claims that he personally tortured prisoners in the Baghdad prison known as Qasr Al Nihaya, the 'Palace of the End'.

This first taste of power did not last long. When Aref turned on his Ba'ath allies, Saddam once again found himself on the run. Arrested in 1964, he escaped in 1966, went into hiding and waited, determined that power would not slip through his grasp a second time. 'When we take over the government,' he told a friend, 'I'll turn this country into a **Stalinist** state.'

After the 1968 coup Saddam's chance arrived. When his patron al-Bakr took over as president and chairman of the new Revolutionary Command Council (RCC), Saddam became the power behind the throne. He took over and expanded the **political police**, and filled them with his own friends and relations. Within two weeks of the coup he had disposed of the new prime minister, taking him to the airport at gunpoint and sending him off to be the new Iraqi ambassador in Morocco.

Throughout the remaining months of that year Saddam expanded his role, taking over new departments and staffing them with his own supporters. In January 1969 he was officially named vice-president, a post he would hold for ten years. The president's health was already declining, leaving Saddam free to carry out the actual business of government, and to take Iraq in whichever direction he himself wanted it to go.

Transforming Iraq

Saddam Hussein's first priority in the weeks and months which followed the July 1968 **coup** was to establish complete control of the country. The new **constitution** allowed for a president, the Revolutionary Command Council, and a National Assembly. All real power, however, rested in the Council, and the man who effectively ran it, Saddam himself. Any would-be opponent in the Council soon found himself a victim of Saddam's other power base, the **political police**.

The Kurds

The Kurds are not Turks, Arabs or Persians, but a people in their own right. There are around 20 million Kurds, almost all of them **Muslim**. They live in a single geographic region which spills across borders into Turkey, Armenia, Iran, Iraq and Syria.

The Iraqi Kurds, who mostly live in the northern third of the country, form around 18 per cent of the country's population. In 1970 they were promised autonomy by the new Iraqi regime of al-Bakr and Saddam Hussein, but rebelled in 1974 – with help from Iran – when the promise was not kept. When Iranian help was withdrawn in 1975, the rebellion collapsed, only to start up again during the Iran-Iraq war. During that war chemical weapons were used against several Kurdish villages – most notably, Halabja, where both mustard gas and cyanide gas were used in 1988 – and thousands of Kurds were forcibly resettled in southern Iraq.

In 1991, at the end of the Gulf War, the Kurds again rose in revolt, but were swiftly defeated when expected Western help failed to arrive. After the defeat, the Western states intervened to set up and enforce a 'safe haven' in northern Iraq. In the 2003 war, many Kurds joined forces with coalition troops to remove Saddam. Some Kurdish activists are now campaigning for independence from Iraq, others for self-rule within the new government.

Throughout 1968, 1969 and beyond, a reign of terror engulfed Iraqi politicians. **Communists**, alleged supporters of Israel, outspoken **Arab nationalists**, suspected **Central Intelligence Agency (CIA)** informants... in fact, anyone who posed a threat to the **Ba'ath's** – and Saddam's – new hold on power was liable to end up in **exile**, in prison, or dead. A new Popular Army, composed entirely of Ba'ath supporters, was created as a counterbalance to the regular army. The regular army was forced to accept Ba'ath officers into its ranks. Those generals not considered reliable suffered dismissal or worse.

The only groups which Saddam chose, for the moment, to indulge, were the **Kurds** and the **Shi'as**. The Kurds were promised substantial **autonomy**, the Shi'as invited into the Ba'ath and given preferential economic treatment. Saddam's treatment of the Shi'as demonstrated one method he intended using in order to remain in power. 'People with full bellies don't make revolutions,' he once told an interviewer.

Iraqi Kurds were often persecuted by Saddam's regime.

Filling bellies

Full bellies cost money. How was Saddam to pay for them? In 1972 he took the risk that none of his predecessors had dared to take: he **nationalized** the foreign-owned Iraqi Petroleum Company, which was responsible for most of the country's oil production. The gamble paid off: Iraqi technicians quickly proved they could run the industry, and the Soviet Union (USSR) said it would buy the country's oil if the West refused to do so. And then, in 1973, Saddam hit the jackpot. The enormous rise in oil prices which followed that year's Arab-Israeli War and subsequent Arab oil **embargo** meant that Iraq was suddenly swimming in money. He had what he needed to transform the country.

The importance of oil

The importance of oil to the world's most highly developed economies cannot be overstated – without it, industry and transport would simply grind to a halt. The Middle East has been a crucial contributor to world oil production for well over half a century, and during that time its importance to Europe, Japan and the USA has grown in leaps and bounds. It is currently believed that the Gulf region contains over two-thirds of the world's oil reserves.

In 1973 – partly as a response to rises in the price of Western food and arms, partly out of a desire to punish the West for its support of Israel in that year's Arab-Israeli War, and partly from a simple desire to make as much money as they could – Arab and other oil producers sharply raised the price of the oil they sold. This produced a global economic slowdown, but it also brought immense wealth to the Middle East.

Since then, some inhabitants of the oil-rich states have seen their living standards rise enormously. Few of them, however, have been granted **democratic** rights. States such as Saudi Arabia, Kuwait and the Gulf Emirates are still tightly controlled by small family groups. Many in the West fear that these regimes will eventually be overthrown by their own peoples, and replaced by anti-Western **Islamic** republics which might choose to cut off the West's oil supply.

In response to this threat, US President Jimmy Carter promised in 1979 that 'any attempt by an outside power to gain control of the Persian Gulf region will be regarded as an assault on the vital interests of the USA, and such an assault will be repelled by any means necessary, including military force.'

Some of this money was ploughed back into economic development. Manufacturing industries of all kinds were set up: chemical and fertilizer plants, brick-making factories, sugar-refining plants. Railways were built, and electric power taken to the villages. Other money was spent on improving health care facilities, and on setting up a basic social security system which helped protect ordinary Iraqis against unemployment, ill health and old age. According to Saddam's biographer Saïd Aburish, by 1978 'Iraq had become a welfare state which was envied by other Arabs and admired by the USSR and the West.'

Economic development: Iraqi engineers constructing a new tunnel in the north of the country.

Expenditure on education soared. One particular target was the ending of illiteracy (inability to read or write), and Saddam's campaign proved so effective that it won an award from UNESCO (the United Nations Educational, Scientific and Cultural Organization). Particular encouragement was given to women, who now found that many more professions were open to them. By the end of the 1970s almost half of Iraq's teachers, and almost a third of its doctors, were women. In 1977 women were allowed into the armed forces, and some even became pilots. This, for the Arab world, was truly revolutionary.

A hunger for arms

But not all of Iraq's new-found wealth was spent on economic development and creating a welfare state. A large and increasing portion was spent on buying weapons from abroad and setting up an arms industry inside Iraq. Saddam was not just interested in the **conventional weapons** he might need to defend Iraq against its neighbours – he was also intent on acquiring the kind of **non-conventional weapons** which would threaten those neighbours and give even the world's most powerful states pause for thought.

Through the 1960s and 1970s his chief supplier of conventional weapons was the Soviet Union, but France also came to play an important role. France sold Saddam his first nuclear reactor, and taught his scientists how to operate it, being well aware that he intended to develop nuclear weapons. Saddam also began gathering the expertise and materials needed for the development of **chemical** and **biological weapons**. The Pfaulder Corporation of Rochester, New York sold him the plans he needed to build his first chemical warfare plant. Later more help was obtained from Italy and West Germany (now part of Germany).

Why were these Western countries so eager to sell dangerous knowledge and materials to a dictator whom they already knew to be both brutal and unscrupulous? Greed was one reason, racism another – the profits were huge and Europeans found it hard to believe that the Iraqis would be able to make sense of the technology they had been sold. There was also the **Cold War** to consider: if the West refused to help Iraq then the Soviets might acquire even more influence in Baghdad. And finally, there was neighbouring Iran. The Shah of Iran was a friend of the West and an important ally of the USA, but he was also the man most responsible for the oil price rises of 1973, which had wreaked such economic havoc around the world. A strong Iraq would help to keep the Shah in check.

An Arab hero

For the moment, Saddam was showing no signs of threatening his neighbours. A long-standing border dispute with Saudi Arabia was resolved, and relations with Kuwait – which had once been part of Iraq and which Iraq had long wished to repossess –

The Shatt al-Arab

Around 385 kilometres (240 miles) to the south-east of Baghdad, Iraq's two great rivers, the Tigris and Euphrates, merge into one. The united river, which flows another 195 kilometres (120 miles) to its outlet in the Persian Gulf, is called the Shatt al-Arab. Over many centuries part of this river has formed the border between Arabs and Persians, Iraq and Iran.

In 1913 the British imposed on the two countries their version of the border, which in some places followed the midstream line of deepest water, and in others the Iranian bank. The Iranians never really accepted this, and continued to demand a simple midstream border. In 1975 Saddam Hussein agreed, on condition that they stopped helping the rebellious Iraqi Kurds. He tried to go back on this deal during the Iran-Iraq War, but reconfirmed it in 1990 after his invasion of Kuwait united the rest of the world against him.

The Shatt al-Arab waterway.

improved. In 1975 Saddam even reached an understanding with Iraq's traditional enemy Iran, and accepted the Iranian demand for a midstream boundary along the Shatt al-Arab in exchange for Iran ending its support for the rebellious Kurds.

Saddam was also making his contribution to Arab unity. The Iraqi Army's performance in the 1973 Arab-Israeli War showed no improvement on its previous outings in 1948 and 1967, but there were other ways to demonstrate a commitment to the Arab cause. Throughout the 1970s the expansion of the Iraqi economy drew in Arabs from other, less fortunate countries, and these migrants reported back on Saddam's success. Here was an Arab country which was spending its wealth on its ordinary people, and which therefore offered an example to other, less generous Arab regimes. Saddam was becoming a hero to the Arab masses. He was slowly becoming more popular in foreign countries than his own.

Self-reliance

'No country which relies on importing weapons is completely independent.'
Saddam Hussein, quoted in Saïd K. Aburish, Saddam Hussein: The Politics of Revenge, *2000*

A family affair

At home, his regime had become noticeably more arbitrary and brutal. He had begun by at least pretending to represent the Ba'ath Party, but now the Ba'ath only existed to carry out his orders. The men who surrounded him, and who filled all the important posts in the government, political police and army, were relations or old friends from the Tikrit region. When any of them behaved badly – as was often the case with his sons Uday and Qussay and his uncle Khairallah – there was no punishment. They could get away with murder, and often did.

Al-Bakr remained president until 1979, but was virtually powerless. After his forced resignation Saddam had a third of the Revolutionary Command Council shot, in person, by the other two-thirds. Little was now heard about the glory of the Ba'ath, much about the glory of Saddam. He was constantly on television, dressed either in military uniforms or the elegant suits which were specially made for him in Switzerland. He was the man who had transformed Iraq, and he soaked up the adulation which his own and other Arab media heaped upon him.

Turning point: attacking Iran

The decision to attack neighbouring Iran in September 1980 was probably the most crucial of Saddam's career. Everything which followed – the long war, virtual bankruptcy, the attack on Kuwait and Iraq's subsequent poverty and isolation – came from this one decision. It put Saddam on a moving train which he never managed to get off.

The spark which lit the fuse was the Iranian Revolution of January 1979. This upheaval, which replaced the **secular**, pro-Western regime of the Shah with the **Islamic** dictatorship of Ayatollah Khomeini, shook the whole **Muslim** world to its foundations. The message was simple, and directed at ordinary people. Your rulers are corrupt, the Iranian revolutionaries told the Arab and other Muslim peoples. They comply with the wishes of the West, they are undemocratic, they live in luxury while the poor go hungry, they have abandoned religious values and tradition for the empty pleasures of the Western way of life. Follow us, they said, follow Islam, and the world can be re-made as God intended.

Arabs and Persians, Sunnis and Shi'as

This message had enough grains of truth to worry most Arab regimes, and particularly Saddam's Iraq. Iran, after all, had always been a problem for the Ba'ath party in Iraq. Most Iranians (or Persians, as they were called until recently) are not Arabs, and the conflict between the two stretches back into ancient times. The Islamic conquest of both countries in the 7th century gave them something in common, but the later **Sunni-Shi'a** split – Iran has usually been led by Shi'as, Iraq by Sunnis – deepened the traditional distrust between them.

There were problems in Saddam's time even before the Iranian Revolution. There was a long-standing border dispute between the two countries along the Shatt al-Arab river, and there was a mutually dangerous situation in the two countries' adjoining southern provinces. The Iranian province of Khuzestan, which was home to most of Iran's oil wealth, had an Arab majority. This gave rise to Iranian fears that Arab Iraq might seek, by force or more subtle methods, to detach Khuzestan from Iran and attach it to Iraq. Across the Shatt al-Arab, the southernmost provinces of Iraq had a Shi'a majority, which gave rise to Iraqi fears that Shi'a Iran might seek to **annex** them in a similar way.

**Muhammad Reza Shah Pahlavi, Shah of Iran (1941–79).
A supporter of the West, he was overthrown by Ayatollah
Khomeini's anti-Western Islamic revolution.**

As 1979 gave way to 1980, Iraq's fears seemed to be coming true.
The new Iranian leader, Ayatollah Khomeini, had lived in
southern Iraq until 1978, when Saddam threw him out to please
the Shah. Khomeini now had his revenge, calling on the Shi'as of
southern Iraq to rebel and rise up against Saddam's regime in
Baghdad. Saddam was already worried by the situation in the
south, and feared that Iranian interference would spark a real
rebellion. Incidents of violent unrest multiplied through 1979–80,
including a near-successful attempt on the life of Deputy Prime
Minister Tariq Aziz. Hundreds of Iraqi Shi'as were executed in
reprisal, but the threat from Iran remained.

Biography – Ayatollah Khomeini

The Ayatollah (1902–89) – a title given to Shi'a Muslim religious leaders – came to prominence in the Iranian city of Qom during the 1950s and 1960s. A lifelong opponent of the Iranian **monarchy** or Shahs, whom he saw as weak followers of the West, Khomeini was arrested and **exiled** in 1963 for opposing land reform and greater rights for women. He settled in Najaf, a Shi'a holy city in southern Iraq, and during the 1970s became a symbol of resistance to the Shah. His teachings were smuggled into Iran on tape cassettes which were then copied thousands of times over.

When the Shah was overthrown early in 1979, Khomeini returned in triumph to create an **Islamic** republic. Religious **censorship** was imposed on education and the media, and women were severely restricted. Tens of thousands of people were executed or imprisoned. In November 1979 Iranian students, angry that the Shah had been allowed into the the USA for medical treatment, seized the US embassy in Tehran and took 90 Americans **hostage**. Most of them were held for over a year. Khomeini's support for the students, and his attempt to incite rebellion in the Gulf states made him an enemy of the USA, whom he regarded as 'The Great Satan'. The eight-year war with Iraq (1980–88) consumed most of the regime's energies and many of its young men, but the Islamic Republic survived. Khomeini himself died in 1989.

Ayatollah Khomeini, leader of the Iranian Revolution.

Giving in to temptation

The two countries exchanged angry words, artillery shells, even air strikes. At some point in the late summer of 1980 Saddam decided on war. What tipped him over the edge? One factor was clearly the level of encouragement and support he was receiving from Iran's other enemies – all those Arab regimes who felt threatened by the Ayatollah's message, and their protector the USA. The Saudis, in particular, seem to have urged Saddam on, reportedly offering him huge financial compensation for any losses he might sustain.

But the most insistent voices urging war were inside his own head. When Saddam heard reports of violent clashes in Khuzestan between the local Arabs and the Iranian authorities he must have felt that destiny was calling. His tanks would roll in, and the Arab population would greet him as their liberator. In a matter of days he could double Iraq's riches and settle for ever the question of who dominated the Persian Gulf. On 22 September 1980 he set the tanks in motion. It proved to be an irretrievable mistake.

Iraqi soldiers at the Khorramshahr front in 1980 at the beginning of the Iran-Iraq conflict.

The Iran-Iraq war

The main thrust of the Iraqi attack in 1980 was across the Shatt al-Arab river and into Khuzestan. The Iranians offered little opposition in open country, but the towns proved a different matter. It took the Iraqis four weeks to subdue the border city of Khorramshahr, and they were forced to a halt outside Abadan, Dezful and further north, in Ahwaz. The **Shi'as** of Khuzestan were not welcoming the Iraqis as liberators; on the contrary, they defended their cities with courage and determination.

Within a week, Saddam must have realized the seriousness of his mistake. On 28 September 1980 he made his first plea for peace, offering to withdraw his forces if Iran recognized the old border along the Shatt al-Arab and promised to stop inciting Iraq's Shi'as to rebellion. The silence from Iran was deafening. The Iraqis continued to make small gains, but by November their advance had stalled. Saddam had nowhere to go.

Iraq and Iran, showing the no-fly zones imposed after the 1991 war.

Trapped in a war

Saddam, with some encouragement from the Saudis, had got himself into this mess, but he needed help to get himself out. He received none, and for one simple reason: peace was in no one else's interest. The Iranians were certainly in no mood to let him off the hook. What incentive did they have? Khuzestan had remained loyal, and this Iranian province was far too big for Saddam to conquer. The feeling in the Iranian capital Tehran was that Saddam had started the war, and that they would eventually finish it, by toppling him and creating a Shi'a **Islamic republic** in Iraq.

A committed enemy

'You are fighting to protect Islam and he [Saddam Hussein] is fighting to destroy Islam. At the moment Islam is confronted by blasphemy [the insulting of God], and you should protect and support Islam... There is no question of peace or compromise, and we shall never have any discussions with them.'
Ayatollah Khomeini, speaking to the Iranian people early in the Iran-Iraq War. Iranian families who lost sons or fathers in the fighting were given a good income by the state, and had a better chance of receiving scarce goods and services

One of Saddam's hopes was that the disruption of Iraqi and Iranian oil supplies to the West and Japan would force the international powers to intervene. But this didn't happen either. The Saudis raised their production to compensate for the lost supplies, so the only sufferers were Iraq and Iran. And the Western powers – including the USA, Britain and France – had no interest in seeing the fighting stopped. They hoped that a long war would weaken both the revolutionary regime in Iran and the ambitious Saddam.

A voluntary arms **embargo** was placed on the two warring countries by the major powers, but the French ignored it, and continued to supply Iraq with state-of-the art weapons such as Exocet-armed Super-Etendard fighter planes. As the war went on, both sides managed to refill their armouries from a variety of sources. The Egyptians helped Iraq with spare parts for their Soviet equipment, and the Saudis passed on US intelligence information and weaponry. Israel and the USA both sold American arms to Iran.

Saddam calls for Iran to give in to his demands, November 1980.

The Americans, according to a State Department memo of 1984, believed that 'victory for either side' in the Iran-Iraq war 'would have far-reaching consequences', and they took steps to help whichever side looked the weaker at any given time. The USA supplied military equipment as well as information to both Iraq and Iran, to help continue a stalemate. The USA was engaging in a divide and conquer strategy that weakened two countries that were threats to US interests in the region.

Inside Iraq

As the months and years went by, the Iraqi economy deteriorated. Oil revenue dropped alarmingly, and Iranian attacks on Iraqi oil wells, refineries and pipelines reduced income still further. Saddam could have told the Iraqi people to tighten their belts for a while, but he was reluctant to do so, mostly for fear of the popular response. Instead, he chose to use up the savings which the country had accumulated over the last few years. When this money had disappeared he turned to borrowing, mostly from Saudi Arabia and Kuwait. He also expanded the **political police** and widened the definition of **treason**. Complaining about Saddam's leadership became punishable by death.

During these years Saddam's immediate circle – the relations and friends who comprised Iraq's ruling body – grew increasingly violent and corrupt. His uncle Khairallah Tulfah created companies to make profits out of the war, and Saddam's wife, in two visits to London and New York City early in 1981, spent millions of US dollars on clothes. The minister of health tried to make his fortune by selling lethal out-of-date **penicillin** to the Iraqi Army, but this was too much even for Saddam. During a cabinet meeting in March 1982 he invited the minister to step outside and shot him dead. The Iraqi media, meanwhile, was busy claiming that Saddam was the last in a long line of great Arab heroes who had fought the Persians.

Iraqi soldiers in 1981 at Khorramshahr, the only major city they captured in the Iran-Iraq war.

The course of the war

Once the Iraqi offensives had been halted in November 1980 the war settled into a long battle of **attrition**, which suited the Iranians better than their opponents. Between September 1981 and May 1982 they took back much of the territory occupied by the Iraqis in their initial attacks, lifted the siege of Abadan, and recaptured Khorramshahr. They achieved these successes by using 'human wave' attacks, in which hundreds of thousands of young men, poorly armed but full of revolutionary enthusiasm, threw themselves against the better-armed Iraqis. Men and boys died in their masses, but the attacks succeeded through sheer weight of numbers. In June 1982 Saddam pulled his army back behind the old border, giving up what little remained of his gains. His requests for a **ceasefire** were met with Iranian demands for huge **reparations** and the removal of Saddam himself.

The war went on. Over the next three years Iranian forces inched their way into Iraqi territory, with each push forward exacting a huge toll in human life. In the south they took the important Fao peninsula; in the north, aided by the Iraqi Kurds, they threatened the important town of Kirkuk.

The oil tanker *Ariadne*, hit by a missile in August 1987 during the Gulf 'Tanker War'.

The Iraqi response to the Iranian tactics was two-fold. On the ground they emphasized defence, using earthworks, minefields and artillery fire-zones to create 'killing fields' for the Iranian infantry. Poison gas was also used, for the first time since the Italian invasion of Abyssinia in 1935 in clear defiance of international law. From 1984 on, the Iraqis employed their superior airpower to attack Iran's major cities and oil trade. The 'War of the Cities' involved both bomber and missile attacks, and the 'Tanker War' was a sustained assault on Iranian installations and shipping in the Gulf. From early 1987, fearful that Iran was gaining the upper hand in the war, the USA gave Iraq considerable assistance in the Gulf. They provided information about Iranian movements and even, on two occasions, launched attacks of their own against Iranian ships and oil platforms. When poison gas was used against the Kurdish town of Halabja in March 1988, killing thousands of civilians, the USA falsely claimed that Iran had carried out the attack.

Gas

'After the Iraqi Army, with American planning assistance, retook the Fao Peninsula [in 1988], a Defence Intelligence Agency Officer, Lieutenant-Colonel Rick Francona, now retired, was sent to tour the battlefield with Iraqi officers. Francona saw zones marked off for chemical contamination, and containers for the drug atropine scattered around, indicating that Iraqi soldiers had taken injections to protect themselves from the effects of gas that might blow back over their positions.'
British journalist Patrick Tyler, offering evidence of Iraqi use of chemical weapons, and American knowledge of the fact

Peace at last

In July 1987 the **United Nations Security Council** finally intervened. Resolution 598 called for a ceasefire and a return to the recognized border between the two countries. Iraq accepted but Iran still wanted reparations and official recognition that Iraq had been the aggressor. However, the military pendulum had now swung back in Iraq's favour, and in the summer of 1988 Ayatollah Khomeini finally accepted the ceasefire. The war had cost as many as a million lives and some 600 billion dollars.

The former US Secretary of State Henry Kissinger famously remarked that it was a pity both sides couldn't lose the Iran-Iraq war. But that, in fact, was exactly what had happened. The two peoples lost: their loved ones killed and maimed, and their standard of living drastically reduced. The two regimes also lost: Iran's revolutionary momentum and Iraq's march towards prosperity and the leadership of the Arab world were both halted in their tracks.

Between wars

By 1988 Iraq's situation was disastrous. The war had wiped out the achievements of the 1970s. The economy, and particularly the oil industry, were in ruins. The country, which had started the war with savings of some US$35 billion, was now US$80 billion in debt (around US$50 billion of which was owed to Saudi Arabia and Kuwait). Economic hardship made the regime increasingly unpopular, and the behaviour of those in power only made matters worse. In October 1988 Saddam's son Uday broke into an official function and shot his father's food-taster dead in front of foreign guests. The motive for this crime – which was swiftly forgiven by Saddam – had something to do with Saddam's abandonment of Uday's mother for another woman. Rumours abounded, and none of them were to the regime's credit.

Saddam, meanwhile, insisted on pretending that the Iran-Iraq war had been a tremendous victory for Iraq, and ordered the construction of an Arch of Triumph featuring enormous crossed swords in Baghdad. While his people struggled to make ends meet he built numerous presidential palaces and imported blue marble floors from Argentina at a cost of US$3000 a square metre.

Friendless

One reason for Saddam's relative lack of concern was his expectation of help from the richer Arab regimes and the West. As far as he believed, Iraq had been defending all of them against the threat of revolutionary Iran, and it seemed only fair that the cost should be shared. He expected the Saudis, Kuwaitis and others to cancel the debts Iraq had incurred during the war, and offer more loans on favourable terms for the rebuilding of the Iraqi economy. In a few years time he would be able to resume his bid for the leadership of the Arab world.

This dream failed to come true. With Iran weakened, Saddam found that his usefulness was over. And not only that. With a million-strong army, Saddam and Iraq were beginning to look as threatening as the Iranians had ever done. The Saudis and Kuwaitis had no interest in Iraq's swift recovery. They refused to cancel the debts.

Nor had Saddam's pursuit of nuclear, **chemical and biological weapons** gone unnoticed, particularly in the USA. The first Bush President – George H.W. Bush – was still willing to do deals with him, but the US **Congress**, increasingly concerned with his **human**

rights record and **non-conventional weapons** programmes, was not. American loans to Iraq were finally suspended in May 1990, but long before then Saddam could not have failed to see which way the wind was blowing.

Biography – George H. W. Bush

Forty-first president of the USA (1989–93). Born in Milton, Massachusetts, Bush (1924–) served as a naval pilot during World War II, and made his fortune in the Texan oil industry during the 1950s and 1960s. A member of the Republican Party, he was appointed US ambassador to the United Nations (1971–3) and China (1974–5) by President Richard Nixon. In 1976–7 he was Director of the American **Central Intelligence Agency (CIA)**.

He served for eight years as Ronald Reagan's vice-president, succeeding him as president in 1989. He was most interested in foreign affairs, negotiating arms reductions with the Soviet Union and intervening in Panama to overthrow the corrupt Noriega regime. In 1990–1 he led the Gulf War **coalition** against Saddam's Iraq, despite his previous willingness to overlook the regime's brutality in the interests of containing Iran.

President George H. W. Bush and General Norman Schwarzkopf ride in a military vehicle in Saudi Arabia, during Operation Desert Shield in November 1990.

The wrong answer

Saddam looked for a way out of the crisis which seemed to be enveloping him. He put himself forward as a champion of the Palestinians and invited the **Palestine Liberation Organization (PLO)** chairman Yasser Arafat to live in Baghdad, hoping that the richer Arab regimes would help him financially rather than risk looking less than enthusiastic about the Palestinian cause. He tried to warn the same regimes that only a strong Iraq could provide a counterbalance to American power in the Gulf now that Soviet power was crumbling. He stepped up his non-conventional weapons programmes, reasoning that intimidation might succeed where persuasion failed. But his arguments fell on deaf ears, and the weapons programmes would take years. He needed something quickly.

Kuwait

Kuwait is a small desert country at the head of the Persian Gulf, sandwiched between Saudi Arabia and Iraq. The population is around 1.8 million, of whom over half are guest workers from elsewhere in the Arab world or south Asia. The al-Sabah family has ruled Kuwait since 1756, firstly as part of the Turkish Empire, then under formal British protection (1914–61), and finally as an independent state.

Oil was discovered in 1938, and after World War II Kuwait became one of the world's leading producers. Recent estimates suggest that the country contains one tenth of the world's total oil reserves.

Since independence there has been some attempt to make the country more democratic, but progress so far has been extremely limited. Only adult male Kuwaiti nationals – some 13 per cent of the population – have a vote, and the parliament they elect remains essentially powerless.

At some point in 1990 Saddam settled on Kuwait as an answer to his problems. Kuwait was not only refusing to defer or cancel the loans, but was also deliberately producing more oil than **OPEC** (Organization of Petroleum Exporting Countries) said it should. As a result, the world price of oil was falling, which made it even harder for Iraq to repay its loans or get its economy running again. As far as Saddam was concerned, this was reason enough for war. And Iraq had long claimed that Kuwait belonged to it, a claim renewed as recently as 1961. Saddam had enough of a case, he reckoned, to make international action unlikely.

Saddam was compounding the mistake he had made in 1980. He decided that Kuwait's oil would give him enough economic power to dominate the whole Middle East. At a stroke, all his economic and political problems would be solved. Who, after all, would stop him? Not the Arab regimes of the Gulf, whose armies were no match for his own. And not, or so he believed, the USA. At a July meeting with April Glaspie, the American ambassador in Baghdad, Saddam was given – or chose to believe that he had been given – the green light for an invasion.

A green light?

On 25 July 1990 the US ambassador to Iraq had an audience with Saddam Hussein which included the following exchange:

Saddam: 'The price of oil at one stage dropped to US$12 a barrel, and a reduction in the modest Iraqi budget of US$6–7 billion is a disaster.'

Ms Glaspie: 'I think I understand this. I have lived here for years. I admire your extraordinary efforts to rebuild your country. I know you need funds. We understand that, and our opinion is that you should have the opportunity to rebuild your country. But we have no opinion on Arab-Arab conflicts like your border disagreement with Kuwait.'

Was this a green light to attack Kuwait? Did Saddam think it was?

Excerpt from a transcript distributed by the Iraqi Government, which may or may not be accurate.

April Glaspie, US ambassador to Iraq in 1990.

Turning point: the invasion of Kuwait

Early in the morning of 2 August 1990 Iraqi troops poured across the Kuwaiti border. By late morning the capital, Kuwait City, had been seized; by the end of the day the whole country was in Iraqi hands. Kuwait was much richer than Iraq, but it was no more democratic. Many of those who lived and worked there did not qualify as citizens, and even citizens came in two classes, first and second. All power rested with the thousand-strong al-Sabah family, which had ruled the area for over 200 years. But if Saddam was expecting a grateful population to welcome his troops as liberators, he was, again, badly mistaken. No Kuwaitis would work with him.

Kuwait's Mina Abdullah oil refinery. Saddam hoped that Kuwait's oil wealth would solve Iraq's economic problems.

The reaction

The international reaction to the invasion was mixed, at least in the beginning. Many ordinary Arabs welcomed Saddam's move as a strike against 'fat cat' Arab regimes and their American protector. The regimes themselves, aware of this feeling among their own populations, waited to see which way the wind was blowing. Beyond the Arab world, there was almost universal condemnation of the invasion. US President George Bush announced that there was 'no place in today's world for this sort of naked aggression', and the other major powers agreed with him. The **United Nations Security Council** passed Resolution 660, which condemned Iraq and called for an immediate withdrawal.

Demonstrators in Iraq's neighbour, Jordan, protest against the deployment of US troops on Arab soil, August 1990.

There was more to this than aggression. The free flow of affordable oil was in jeopardy. The Bush Administration, with the enthusiastic support of Prime Minister Margaret Thatcher's government in Britain, put immediate pressure on Saudi Arabia to allow the stationing of Western troops on its soil. The first units arrived as early as 8 August. The stated aims of their **deployment** were an Iraqi withdrawal from Kuwait, the restoration of the ruling family, and the protection of stability in the Gulf region.

Saddam visits his troops in Iraqi-occupied Kuwait, October 1990.

Saddam had trapped himself again. He made a vague promise of withdrawal to the other Arab states, provided his troops were given safe conduct and the original invasion was not condemned. When this offer was spurned, he formally **annexed** Kuwait as Iraq's 19th province. A few days later he offered to withdraw once more, but only if the Israelis withdrew from the occupied Palestinian West Bank and Gaza Strip. This 'linkage' of the two issues was popular among ordinary Arabs, but ignored by their governments. Saddam then announced that the Western civilians he had rounded up in Kuwait were now **hostages** against a Western attack. The women and children were held in Baghdad hotels, the men taken to airfields to form 'human shields' against bombing.

Invasion

'When I looked out of my window I could see smoke billowing in the distance and could hear machine-gun fire. We didn't realize what was going on until 6 a.m., when a statement was made by the Kuwaiti Defence Department. After that, there was a mass panic with people ringing their relatives to see if everything was all right. I went into the city at 10 a.m. Iraqi troops were manning all key government offices. Tanks were patrolling the city. The streets are now deserted and people are too frightened to go out.'
A Kuwaiti journalist describes the day of the invasion

Building a coalition

Through the rest of August and into September 1990, the USA was busy building a **coalition** against Iraq. This was necessary for both military and political reasons: the USA needed bases in the Middle East to operate from and it needed to show the world that its actions had international support. Some states, like Britain, were happy to join the coalition, while others expected to be rewarded for their participation, in one form or another. The USA gave a lot of financial assistance to Egypt, Syria and Turkey, and stopped criticizing the Chinese government's treatment of its own citizens. There were also threats. The small Arab state of Yemen, which had **abstained** on the vote for Resolution 660 in the Security Council, was told by the US Secretary of State James Baker that this was the most expensive vote it would ever cast. The implication was clear – states who opposed the USA would receive no future economic help.

The UN Security Council votes unanimously to condemn Iraq's invasion of Kuwait.

Through the remaining months of 1990, as stories of torture and murder began seeping out of occupied Kuwait, the build-up of coalition forces in Saudi Arabia went on. Early in November the USA announced that an air campaign against Iraq would start in mid-January; Saddam responded by threatening to launch missiles against Israel and to set the Kuwaiti oil wells ablaze. On 29 November the UN Security Council passed Resolution 678, which authorized members 'to use all necessary means' against Iraq if it failed to withdraw its forces from Kuwait. Saddam was persuaded by **PLO** chairman Yasser Arafat to release his Western hostages, but otherwise remained defiant. At 2 a.m. on 17 January 1991 the first coalition planes took off from their Saudi bases and headed for Iraq. 'Operation Desert Storm' had begun.

Turning point: Gulf War of 1991

The air war lasted five weeks. Its stated aims were the destruction of Iraqi morale and the Iraqi capacity to resist. Its unstated aim was to reduce the casualties of a later **coalition** ground attack to an absolute minimum, even if this meant a large number of Iraqi civilian deaths. Much emphasis was placed on the new **'smart bombs'** and how accurate they were. These bombs were, in fact, only 20 per cent accurate, and most of the bombs dropped were of the old, not-so-smart kind, frequently missing their targets with devastating effect. Several schools and hospitals were hit, and on 13 February 1991 over 400 civilians were killed in a Baghdad bomb shelter.

The Iraqis had little defence against this assault from the air, and at this stage Saddam's only real hope lay in the growing body of international opinion opposed to the coalition's conduct of the conflict. Two days after the original invasion of Kuwait the **United Nations** had imposed economic **sanctions** against Iraq, which included both foods and medicines, and it seemed to many people that both sanctions and air war were targeting the innocent rather than the guilty. But both continued. By 24 February 1991 – the day the ground war began – coalition planes had flown around 100,000 sorties, dropped 85,000 tons of explosives, and caused damages in the region of $110 billion. Thousands of civilians had been killed.

Retreating Iraqi vehicles destroyed from the air, March 1991.

The ground war

Countries cannot be liberated or conquered by air attacks alone – only ground troops can take control of the ground. The ground war which began on 24 February 1991 lasted slightly less than 100 hours. While some coalition forces reoccupied Kuwait, others attacked across the desert towards the Euphrates River, trapping a large part of the Iraqi army between them. Unable to move, the columns of Iraqi vehicles were repeatedly attacked by coalition planes. Some pilots called it a 'turkey shoot', while others, according to some reports, were so disgusted by the slaughter that they refused to continue with the bombing. Meanwhile, more than half of Kuwait's oil wells had been set alight by the retreating Iraqis, and were blackening the sky above the desert. At 8 a.m. on 28 February, with the enemy clearly beaten, President Bush ordered a **ceasefire**. The coalition forces had lost fewer than 200 soldiers, the Iraqis probably tens of thousands.

Baghdad at war

There was no electric power in Baghdad because all the power stations had been knocked out in the first days of the bombing. The people of the city huddled in darkness. The stench of decaying meat hung over the more prosperous districts as steaks in carefully-stocked freezers slowly rotted...

The restaurants on Sadoun Street in central Baghdad were shuttered and empty, replaced by kerbside cooking fires fuelled by branches torn from the trees by the bombs. Over everything there hung the yellow haze of a winter fog.'
from Andrew and Patrick Coburn's biography, Saddam Hussein, an American Obsession

But Saddam Hussein was still in power. Why did President Bush prevent his forces from advancing on Baghdad, and removing him? For one thing, the Bush administration was uncertain how many American casualties the American public would put up with. For another, the Arab coalition partners had never agreed to the removal of Saddam, and were still utterly opposed to such action. However, what really worried the Bush administration were the consequences of such a removal. Take away Saddam and Iraq would probably collapse into chaos, or even disintegrate completely. And the USA still needed a strong Iraq to counter the continuing threat from Iran.

The USA needs a strong Iraq

'The trick here was to damage his offensive capability without weakening Iraq to the point that a vacuum was created, and destroying the balance between Iran and Iraq, further destabilizing the region for years.'
President George H. W. Bush in 1990

The aftermath

Despite its own reluctance to remove Saddam, the Bush administration constantly called on the Iraqi people to do so. But the Americans had no real desire for a mass uprising. What they wanted was for a small group inside the Iraqi political, military or security **elites** to mount a successful **coup** against Saddam. With him gone, they would hopefully have someone more reasonable to deal with. And there would be no huge social upheaval, just a change of faces at the top. In those circumstances, Iraq would remain a credible counterforce to Iran.

However, the Bush administration got a huge social upheaval after all. On 5 March 1991, just two days after the coalition generals had officially accepted the Iraqi surrender, the Shi'as of southern Iraq rose up in revolt. Saddam's military and **political police** were thrown out of the southern cities. The Shi'as' success inspired the Kurds to rise in their turn, and soon over 60 per cent of Iraq was in rebel hands. It seemed, for a short while, as if Saddam would be brought down by his own people.

But he still had huge, heavily-armed forces to deploy against the poorly-armed rebels. Terrified Shi'a civilians who asked the coalition forces for help were refused, and Saddam's Republican Guard troops were allowed through American lines to attack the rebels. The last thing the Bush administration wanted was a Shi'a-ruled Iraq, which they could only imagine as a second Iran.

Saddam's revenge on the Shi'as was predictably savage. Many more were killed in his suppression of their revolt than died in the war which preceded it – some estimates run as high as 300,000 fatalities. Saddam also used his helicopter gunships on the Kurds, forcing thousands of them to seek the safety of the Turkish border. It was here that the Western media caught up with them, and television pictures of the Kurds' suffering forced the Western governments to create a safe haven in northern Iraq, where Saddam's gunships were not allowed to fly. Eventually, they created a similar no-fly zone in the south, which at least limited the damage the regime could inflict on the Shi'as. The war was over, but only those questions surrounding Kuwait had been answered. The questions surrounding Iraq and its leader remained.

Some Kurdish refugees wash in the river, while others wait to cross the footbridge into Turkey, April 1991.

Containment of Saddam and Iraq

When the Gulf War ended in the spring of 1991 Iraq and its people found themselves in terrible shape. The **coalition** bombing campaign had destroyed much of the country's **infrastructure** – its bridges, roads and railways, oil and electricity lines, drainage and sewage systems. The economic **embargo** imposed the previous summer had already created shortages of essentials like medicine and food. These would have been crucial blows to an economy in good health, but Iraq's had already been severely weakened by the long war with Iran.

In neighbouring Kuwait, firefighters gradually extinguished more than 700 oil wells set ablaze by the retreating Iraqis. However, a dense cloud of pollution hung over the northern Gulf for the rest of the year, causing significant health problems for the local populations. Black snow even fell out of the sky in distant Afghanistan.

Weapons of Mass Destruction (WMD)

Weapons of mass destruction are generally divided into three types – nuclear, chemical and biological. Nuclear weapons make use of the energy released when atoms are either split or fused together. They range from so-called 'dirty bombs', which can spread lethal radiation, to the sort of highly sophisticated and incredibly destructive explosive devices which the world's leading military powers possess. **Chemical weapons** are synthetic poisons, usually in the form of gases. **Biological weapons** employ nature's deadliest organisms like lethal viruses and bacteria, usually in a highly concentrated form. All three types can be delivered over long distances by bomber or ballistic missile. They can also be taken to their targets by individuals or small groups in a variety of ways.

Only one state – the USA – has ever used nuclear weapons, against Japan in 1945, though many other nations have them. Several states have used chemical weapons, including both sides in World War I, Britain in Iraq during the 1920 revolt, Italy during its conquest of Abyssinia in 1935–6, and Iraq against the Kurds and Iranians in the 1980s. The use of weapons of mass destruction is outlawed by the Geneva Convention of 1925, but their production, possession and sale are not.

The man most responsible for all these disasters was still in power. The US-led coalition, having decided against removing him, now had no choice but to contain him. His country would be weakened, his military movements circumscribed, his **weapons of mass destruction** taken away, and his every move watched. This policy of containment had three essential parts. The first was a continuing Western military presence, the second a **United Nations**-conducted programme of weapons inspection, the third a continuation of economic **sanctions** until such time as the weapons were removed.

US, British and French planes remained in the area. They enforced no-fly zones (areas in which Iraqi military flights were not allowed) in the northern third and southern half of the country. Whenever the Western powers thought Saddam needed a reminder of his obligations, their planes would launch attacks against military targets in Iraq. As the decade wore on, these attacks became more frequent, and the definition of a military target grew more elastic. On those occasions when Saddam showed real signs of defiance – as, for example, when he massed troops on the Kuwaiti border in October 1994 – American troops were airlifted to the Middle East in large numbers.

Weapons inspection

The second part of the containment policy, as spelt out in **UN Security Council** Resolution 687, was weapons inspection. Iraq was supposed to give **UNSCOM** (the United Nations Special Commission) a list of the weapons of mass destruction (nuclear, chemical and biological) which it possessed. UNSCOM's inspectors would then take as long as they needed to check that the list was accurate. Once this was done, the weapons would be destroyed, and **monitoring devices** installed to prevent their secret recreation at a later date.

UNSCOM inspectors measure the nerve gas in an Iraqi container in 1991.

UN Resolution 687

- 'Iraq must accept the destruction or removal of all chemical and biological weapons, and ballistic [guided] missiles with ranges greater than 150 kilometres (93 miles). A similar procedure applies to nuclear material. The UN will monitor and verify destruction and removal.'
- 'Iraq is liable for damages arising from its invasion of Kuwait payable out of its oil revenues.'
- 'The embargo on food is removed. Other sanctions will be lifted after weapons are removed. An arms embargo is maintained.'

Extracts from UN Resolution 687, 3 April 1991.

From the outset, the Iraqis demonstrated a reluctance to provide the 'full, final and complete disclosure' which was required. The UNSCOM inspectors were forced to dig for the information. They arrived unannounced at suspected factories and research centres, sifted through aerial photographs and other detection devices, questioned Iraqis who were now living outside the country, and pored through the records of what Iraq had purchased abroad. Each time a new facility was discovered, the Iraqis would reluctantly admit to its existence, but deny that there were any more. When they showed more stubbornness than usual, the USA and the UK would use cruise missiles on suspected sites. Slowly but surely, or so the inspectors believed, the truth was emerging. By 1995, UNSCOM director Rolf Ekeus believed that most, if not all, of Iraq's significant secret weapons programmes had been discovered and stopped. Economic sanctions, he hoped, could soon be removed.

Then, in the summer of that year, Saddam's sons-in-law Hussein and Saddam Kamel fled to neighbouring Jordan. Both men had held high office in Iraq, and they brought details of several important programmes involving nuclear, chemical and biological weapons which UNSCOM had failed to uncover. The inspectors were told to start again.

Sanctions
It was intended that the economic sanctions imposed against Iraq in 1990 would be lifted when UNSCOM declared Saddam weapon-free. This did not happen, so the sanctions remained in place, despite the immense suffering they were causing, and the

outrage which this suffering produced among many in the Arab world and the West. Some argued that Saddam's refusal to cooperate fully with UNSCOM – and his rejection of Security Council resolutions designed to get food and medicine to ordinary Iraqis – made him completely responsible for the suffering. Others argued that the West knew very well that Saddam would not cooperate, but imposed the sanctions anyway.

Whoever was responsible, the suffering was widespread. UNICEF (the United Nations International Children's Emergency Fund) estimated that in one year – 1993 – between 80,000 and 100,000 children died in Iraq as a direct result of the sanctions. But when US Secretary of State Madeleine Albright was asked, on US television in 1996, about the effect of sanctions on the Iraqi people, she replied that 'the pain was worth it.'

Iraqi women protest against sanctions outside the UN headquarters in Baghdad in 1993.

In 1996 Saddam accepted new UN Resolution 986, which allowed Iraq to sell enough oil to buy food, medicines and other basic needs. But in practice even this failed to address the humanitarian issues at stake. Each and every item Iraq wanted to import was scrutinized by a sanction committee, and anything which the Iraqi military might use – from pencils to computers to fertilizers – was forbidden, even when the intended users were almost certainly civilian. Iraq's economy continued to decline. To take just one example: as water treatment plants broke down for lack of spare parts, so water was once again carried in skin bags on the backs of donkeys. According to the World Health Organization, Iraq had been 'relegated to the pre-industrial age'.

Turning point: suspending weapons inspection

In July 1997 Rolf Ekeus resigned as Director of **UNSCOM**, and was replaced by Richard Butler, an Australian diplomat. Butler was determined that UNSCOM would carry out its work thoroughly, even if that meant confronting Saddam head-on. He gave his subordinate Scott Ritter, an ex-US Marine, permission to make all the surprise raids he considered necessary.

The Iraqis responded accordingly. UNSCOM vehicles were deliberately blocked; inspection teams were held up at factory front gates while incriminating evidence disappeared out the back. More and more premises were suddenly reclassified as 'presidential palaces', which UNSCOM was not allowed to visit. When Butler challenged these restrictions at his regular meetings with Deputy Prime Minister Tariq Aziz he was treated to 'a mixture of bluster, brazenly inept lies, and thinly-veiled threats of violence'. In October 1997 he reported to the **UN Security Council** that Iraq was in breach of its obligations under Resolution 687.

UN chief weapons inspector Richard Butler shakes hands with Iraqi Deputy Prime Minister Tariq Aziz in July 1998 after their first round of disarmament talks.

The end of the coalition
The **coalition** which had been formed in 1990 to reverse the invasion of Kuwait was now little more than a memory. Arab states such as Saudi Arabia, Egypt and Syria were still wary of Saddam, but they were more frightened of their own people, many of whom continued to regard the anti-Western, anti-Israeli

Saddam as an Arab hero. These states were not willing to take military action against Saddam for defying UNSCOM. On the Security Council, three of the five permanent members – France, Russia and China – were also opposed to action. France and Russia both wanted an end to **sanctions**. For one thing, they were owed large amounts of money by Iraq; for another, they believed that sanctions were turning ordinary Iraqis and their fellow-Arabs against the West, and in that sense actually strengthening Saddam. Only the USA and Britain continued to support a hard line against Saddam, insisting that sanctions should remain in place until UNSCOM was completely satisfied.

UNSCOM technicians install a monitoring camera in an Iraqi factory.

The end of weapons inspection

Saddam interpreted the Security Council's lack of unity as weakness, and decided to go on challenging UNSCOM's authority. He expelled UNSCOM's American members (claiming – correctly, as it later turned out – that some of them were using the job to spy for their own country and for Israel), and only agreed to their return when President Clinton ordered a huge build-up of US forces in the Gulf. Saddam's continued refusal to allow access to the so-called presidential palaces created another crisis in February 1998. This was only defused when UN Secretary-General Kofi Annan negotiated a compromise solution – UNSCOM inspectors would only be allowed into these 'palaces' when accompanied by diplomats from neutral countries.

Saddam Hussein reading in his Baghdad office in November 1998, as tension builds between Iraq and the UN. Three weeks later, Iraq was bombed by US and British air forces.

Saddam continued to push and UNSCOM to push back. In the spring of 1998 a rocket grenade was 'accidentally' fired into UNSCOM headquarters in Baghdad; in July the inspectors uncovered documents which proved, yet again, that the Iraqis had lied to them about a **weapons of mass destruction** programme (in this case, involving VX nerve gas). Despite this, Saddam demanded an official announcement from UNSCOM that Iraq had disarmed. When Butler refused, Saddam suspended the inspectors' work. The USA and Britain responded by ordering another build-up of forces in the Gulf, and UNSCOM personnel were finally withdrawn from Iraq in early December 1998.

Hard work

'Every step in disarmament, every discovery and destruction of weapons and the means to make them, was achieved in the face of Iraqi concealment, deception, lying, and threats.'
Richard Butler, executive chairman of UNSCOM

Between 16 and 20 December 1998 the US and British air forces carried out 'Operation Desert Fox', a sustained bombing campaign against Iraq. There was no international support for this campaign, and no apparent military purpose behind it. It was intended as punishment. Through the years that followed such attacks were sporadically repeated, sometimes with a specific military end in mind, sometimes for no other reason than to remind Saddam that he was helpless in the face of Western strength. Sanctions were still preventing him from acquiring what he needed to rebuild his military forces and develop new weapons of mass destruction, even as they condemned his people to poverty and sickness. Containment, though cruel, seemed to be working.

Biography – Tariq Aziz

A Catholic Arab, Tariq Aziz (1936–) was born in Mosul. He joined the **Ba'ath** Party as a teenager and worked as a journalist from 1958. Between 1963 and 1969 he edited the main Ba'ath Party newspapers, and in 1972 he joined the regime's ruling body, the Revolutionary Command Council. He remained there until 2003, serving, at different times, as minister of information, foreign minister and deputy-prime minister. In 1980 he was the target of a failed assassination attempt.

Over his last fifteen years in office he often functioned as Saddam's ambassador to the world, negotiating with the UN and its weapons inspectors, and explaining the regime's positions and policies to the world's press. Shortly after the end of the 2003 war in Iraq, he gave himself up to the US-led coalition.

Tariq Aziz was one of Saddam's closest colleagues for over 30 years.

Reporting the conflict between Saddam and the West

The Western media have often simplified or otherwise distorted the truth about the Middle East. Arabs have been confused with **Muslims**, although many Arabs are not Muslims and many Muslims are not Arabs. And this 'Arab-Muslim' **stereotype** which has filled much of the Western media has been almost completely negative. These people, according to the stereotype, all hated Israel. They raised the price of oil and sometimes threatened to choke off the supply altogether. They despised the West and called the USA the 'Great Satan'. They treated their women badly. They deserved to be looked down on, and they were.

For many years, Iraq was virtually ignored by the Western media. Saddam, and the discovery that Iraq's oil reserves were much more extensive than previously thought, changed all that. Iraq was suddenly important, both as a threat and as a source of possible wealth.

Reporting the Gulf War

The Gulf War was the first major war carried around the world by global TV networks like the USA's CNN and Britain's BBC. Their coverage, which even included reports from inside Iraq, was fuller and fairer than the coverage offered by the Iraqi media, but it was far from completely full or fair. Negative 'Arab-Muslim' images were now applied to Saddam and Iraq, but withheld, for the time being, from those 'Arab-Muslims' fighting on the side of the West. The Saudis and Kuwaitis became 'good Arabs', and it was rarely mentioned that their governments were as undemocratic as Saddam's.

When it came to reporting the actual war, there was an air of unreality. The live coverage of bombing raids was stunning, but seemed more like a video game than a real war, one in which there were no real victims. And when the ground war began many Western journalists bitterly complained that the military authorities were denying them access to areas of conflict. The sparse film and photographs of the Mittlah Ridge carnage which did emerge – mostly of vehicle crews burnt alive in their cabs – were truly shocking. Unlike the rest of the visual media's vast output, these images managed to bring home the flesh-and-blood reality of the war.

This 1998 photo shows president Clinton discussing a recent newspaper editorial about Iraq's use of poison gas.

No news is bad news

Between the end of the Gulf War in 1991, and the **terrorist** attack on the New York World Trade Centre in September 2001, Iraq and Saddam were often out of the news. Moments of crisis, like Saddam's dismissal of the UN weapons inspectors, provided headlines for the newspapers and lead items for TV news programmes, but the slow grind of **sanctions** was only mentioned if someone important chose to make an issue of it on a particular day. Similarly, the sporadic American and British bombing attacks on Iraq became less newsworthy with each passing raid, and by the end of the 1990s a keen follower of the news would have had good reason to believe that they had stopped. In fact, they were still going on. But they were no longer news.

Prelude to war

On 11 September 2001 members of the **Islamic terrorist** Al-Qaeda group hijacked four civilian flights in the north-eastern USA. Two of these planes were flown into the World Trade Centre in New York City and one into the US Defence Department's Pentagon headquarters in Washington DC. The fourth plane crashed in rural Pennsylvania, probably as a result of passenger resistance to the hijackers. Over 3000 people lost their lives as a result of these terrible actions.

The ruins of New York City's World Trade Centre, destroyed by terrorist attack on 11 September 2001.

There was nothing to connect Saddam or Iraq with these attacks. US Vice-President Dick Cheney, when asked in September 2001 whether he believed Saddam had played any part in them, answered with a simple 'no'. Almost all expert opinion agreed with him. The only thing that Saddam and Al-Qaeda had in common was a hatred of the USA; in most other respects they seemed worlds apart. Saddam was a **secular Arab nationalist**, Al-Qaeda a group of religious fanatics. Over the following year the Western **intelligence** agencies scoured the globe for any evidence of a significant connection, and came up with nothing.

In the meantime, US President George W. Bush (son of former President George Bush) had announced that his country was now engaged, along with as many allies as it could gather, in a 'War on Terrorism'. The first targets of that war were the multi-national members of Al-Qaeda and the Taliban regime in Afghanistan which had given them training facilities and a home. By the end of the year the Taliban had been removed from power and

Al-Qaeda scattered. However, the leadership of Al-Qaeda remained at large, and was believed to pose a continuing threat.

Homing in on Iraq

In January 2002 George W. Bush widened the scope of the 'War on Terrorism' to include a group of states – Iran, Iraq and North Korea – which he collectively termed an 'axis of evil'. Over the days and weeks that followed it became apparent that Iraq was the next candidate for American punitive action. Much was made of Saddam's **weapons of mass destruction**, and of two facts in particular: that he had used such weapons against his own people, and that it was now almost four years since the inspectors had been pulled out of Iraq. Who knew, the Americans asked, what horrors he was making now?

There had been general agreement among the Western powers that the **UN** inspectors should return, and that Saddam should be forced to give up any new weapons of mass destruction which he had stockpiled. The Bush administration now insisted that Saddam himself had to go, and quickly, before he either used his weapons of mass destruction or handed them over to terrorists. It argued that Saddam had defied numerous UN resolutions, and could not be allowed to keep doing so. It argued that the Iraqi people would welcome their liberation from a cruel dictatorship.

The administration's critics, both inside and outside the USA, were not convinced by these arguments. They argued that even if Saddam did have weapons of mass destruction – which they doubted – he had no means of using them, and was extremely unlikely to hand them over to terrorists. They pointed out that many other countries beside Iraq had defied the UN, and that if the administration really cared about the people of Iraq it would lift the economic **sanctions** which were causing such hardship. The Bush administration's real reasons for intervening, according to the critics, were two-fold. They wanted to show the American people that they were taking action against one of the USA's enemies, and they wanted to get their hands on Iraq's huge reserves of oil. Such action, the critics said, would widen and deepen existing **Muslim** resentment of the West, and make it harder to win the War on Terrorism.

The UN takes a hand

In September 2002 American preparations for war were interrupted by Saddam's announcement that he would accept the return of the weapons inspectors. After several weeks of

No delivery

'Of course, now the inspectors have left Iraq, we don't know what happens inside factories. But that doesn't really matter, since you have to bring rockets out, and fire them on test stands. This is detectable. No one has detected any evidence of Iraq doing this. Iraq continues to declare its missile tests, normally around eight to twelve a year. Our radar detects the tests, we know what the characteristics are, and we know there's nothing to be worried about.'
UNSCOM inspector Scott Ritter, claiming in 2002 that even if Iraq had created chemical, biological or nuclear warheads, it could not have developed the missiles needed to deliver them

argument and debate, on 8 November the **UN Security Council** unanimously passed Resolution 1441. This required the Iraqis to list all the weapons of mass destruction they had, and to allow the returning weapons inspectors to search wherever they wished. The resolution stopped short, however, of considering any Iraqi obstruction – or 'material breach' of the resolution – as an automatic trigger for war. It was agreed that another resolution would be needed to justify military action if such a 'material breach' occurred.

Over the next few weeks the inspectors resumed their work and the Iraqis produced the required list. The inspectors reported that the Iraqis were cooperating with them, but the list – according to both the inspectors and the US Government – was considerably less than complete. The USA and Britain went back to their argument that any delay in disarming Saddam and Iraq would be dangerous, and began pushing, early in February 2003, for another UN resolution to legitimize an invasion of Iraq. These diplomatic moves were reinforced by a steady build-up of the nations' military forces on the borders of Iraq.

This pressure was resisted by other leading governments – most notably, those of France, Germany, Russia and China – and the French government publicly promised to **veto** any resolution which was designed as a trigger for war. This group of governments – as opinion polls taken at the time made clear – were supported by the vast majority of their own citizens, and by majorities in most other countries, including Britain. The USA and Britain now had to decide whether they were prepared to go it alone, without UN approval, significant international support, or even the certainty that such action would be legal under international law. Most international lawyers thought that it would not be.

They decided to do so. On 20 March 2003 American and British forces launched the war to remove Saddam from power. They and their media talked of a **coalition**, but this was slightly misleading. In 1991, many countries had played an active role in the coalition which went to war. In 2003, the war effort – the troops, the equipment, the money, the determination – was overwhelmingly American and British.

Biography – George W. Bush

Forty-third president of the USA (2001–). Born in New Haven, Connecticut, on 6 July 1946. George W. Bush attended Yale University, and, like his father George Bush, made his fortune in the Texan oil industry. Also a Republican, he served for five years as governor of Texas (1995–2000), and won the presidential election of 2000, defeating the Democrat candidate Al Gore in what many regarded as an unfair vote.

Once in office he was criticised for refusing to join international initiatives, such as attempts to halt environmental decline. However, in the aftermath of September 11 he was able to create a wide coalition of other nations for the military overthrow of the Taliban government in Afghanistan. When it came to Iraq, however, this coalition began to dissolve, with many critics claiming that his administration was using the 'War on Terrorism' as a cover for the pursuit of its own interests. After the fall of Saddam's regime, his administration faced further criticism over the continuing violence and disorder in Iraq.

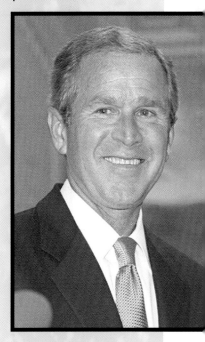

George W. Bush, whose father was president during the Gulf War of 1991.

Turning point: the war in Iraq

In the Gulf War of 1991, the forces of the American-led **coalition** had launched a long bombing campaign against Iraqi air defences before launching a ground invasion. This was not considered necessary in 2003, because years of sporadic American and British bombing had prevented the Iraqis from creating any meaningful defences. This time the air and land assaults began simultaneously.

The aims of the air war were both military and psychological. On the military side, they were almost completely successful. Any Iraqi ground force which tried to interrupt the progress of the coalition ground forces received an instant and usually terminal attack from the air. And attacks on the Iraqi military communications soon made it almost impossible for the regime to coordinate its forces. On the psychological level, success was harder to judge. The US military leadership used the phrase 'shock and awe' to describe the intensity of its air attacks on Baghdad; the intention was to frighten Saddam's regime and army into submission. However, the coalition leadership's determination to limit civilian casualties obviously made it more difficult to terrorize the regime. After all, both civilians and leaders lived in the same city.

Protest

In the weeks leading up to the war there were enormous demonstrations against the expected American and British military action. These took place in many cities around the world, including some in America and Britain. Some people protested because they believed that military action should never be used to settle disputes, others because they believed that not enough effort had been made to settle matters peacefully in this particular case.

These protests did not dissuade the American and British governments from taking military action, but they did perhaps make those governments more careful than they might have been to minimize Iraqi civilian casualties. Once action was underway, some American and British opponents of the war thought it right to end their protests and support their troops, but others continued to oppose the war, and to demand that those who had started it should not profit from their victory.

While the coalition's planes patrolled the skies and bombed Iraqi forces, the coalition ground forces crossed the border and advanced into Iraq. The British headed for Iraq's second city of Basra, 65 kilometres (40 miles) to the north on the Shatt al-Arab waterway. The Americans headed north towards Nasiriyah on the Tigris. From here they sent two main armies further north towards Baghdad, one following the Tigris, the other advancing across the Mesopotamian plain to follow Iraq's other great river, the Euphrates. Neither British nor American land forces met any significant resistance in this early phase. The Iraqis knew that any attempt to make a stand in the open desert would bring the coalition's air forces down on them.

Angry Iraqis gather in a Baghdad street after a US bomb or missile kills at least fifteen civilians on 26 March 2003.

Resistance and collapse

If Saddam had any **weapons of mass destruction**, he did not use them to save his regime. Resistance, when it began, came from small determined units of Iraqi soldiers in the cities. The British spent several days securing complete control of the small port town of Umm Qasr, and did not even try to enter Basra, preferring simply to encircle the city. The Americans encountered opposition in and around those cities, like Nasiriyah and Najaf, which lay on their route to Baghdad. The level of Iraqi resistance was not high – at this stage, more coalition troops had been killed by accidents and each other than by Iraqis – but it was more than had been expected. As the war went into its second week it seemed as if the coalition advance had suffered a setback, and that taking Baghdad might prove difficult if the Iraqi forces chose to fight for their capital street by street. In such a situation, the coalition leaders knew they would find it hard to limit civilian casualties, and their aim of winning over Iraqi public opinion would become that much more difficult.

In the event, this proved the low point of the coalition's war. By the end of the second week the American forces were closing in on Baghdad from two sides, and on 4 April they took control of the city's airport. The Iraqi capital was still being bombed on a regular basis, and the regime's ability to command its troops was increasingly in doubt. On 5 April one American unit penetrated to the heart of the city, while others tightened their grip on the roads leading in and out of the city. On the following day the British finally took control of Basra. Sporadic Iraqi resistance continued in Baghdad for another two days, but then, on 9 April, Saddam Hussein's regime suddenly crumbled. Its leaders and spokespersons disappeared and the people took to the streets. Statues of Saddam were pulled from their pedestals.

A statue of Saddam Hussein, toppled by Iraqis with a little help from US troops, 9 April 2003.

In almost three weeks of war, around 10,000 Iraqi combatants and 2,500 Iraqi civilians had been killed. The Americans had lost 105 soldiers, the British 32.

Embedding

During the 2003 war in Iraq many journalists were 'embedded' - that is to say, they were attached to particular military units for the duration of the conflict. This, in effect, gave them front row seats to the war, and so made it easier for them to report the thoughts and feelings of coalition troops. However, it also made it easier for the military to control what those journalists did and did not see, and for this reason many of their colleagues preferred to operate independently of the military. Either way, reporting the war proved a dangerous business. Ten journalists lost their lives during the three week campaign.

Aftermath

At first there was no sign of Saddam himself, or of the regime's other senior figures. There were rumours that Saddam had been killed in a bombing raid, and counter-rumours that he had been seen both inside and outside Baghdad. Since he was reported to use several look-alike 'doubles', it was hard to confirm or deny any of these rumours. His cousin Ali Hassan al-Majid – who had been given the name 'Chemical Ali' after ordering several gas attacks against the Kurds in 1987–8 – was reportedly killed by a bombing raid in Basra, and Foreign Minister Tariq Aziz gave himself up, but most of Saddam's closest allies remained unaccounted for, and were presumably on the run. One thing, though, was certain. The group of men who had ruled Iraq with such brutality for over a quarter of a century had been removed from power.

As the rest of the country was slowly brought under coalition control – the cities of Kirkuk and Mosul fell on April 11–12, Saddam's hometown of Tikrit on April 13 – international arguments about the legitimacy and conduct of the war turned into international arguments concerning peace and Iraq's long-term future. The countries which had opposed the Anglo-American war now demanded that the United Nations was given a key role in overseeing the country's political and economic recovery, but the USA insisted on keeping the leading role for itself. In May 2003, veteran US diplomat Paul Bremer was installed as Iraq's chief administrator.

Iraq after Saddam

In the months that followed the war – a time of great hardship for most ordinary Iraqis – it was clear that the political and economic reconstruction of the country would be neither easy nor quick. The war had been won, and Iraq liberated, but did the Iraqi people want what their liberators planned for them? As the weeks went by, and violence against British and American troops continued, it became increasingly clear that many of them did not.

The occupying troops were faced with a variety of tasks. Primary among them were restoring law and order, as well as basic services such as water and electricity, to the Iraqi citizens. Roads and buildings – including hospitals and schools – had to be rebuilt. Most important, the occupying forces needed to develop a plan to hand control of Iraq back to its people.

So far, so good

'I did not agree with the reason for the war. I don't believe Bush's excuse that we had illegal weapons. But I am happy to see the end of Saddam Hussein. I am a Shi'a Muslim, and he did terrible things to the Shi'as. But while the Americans and British talk about a "free Iraq" it does not feel free. It will not be until the armies have gone.'
Mukhallad al-Sinwai, a 36 year-old Iraqi pharmacist from Nasiriyah

However, things were not so simple. Although most Iraqis had been anti-Saddam, they were not necessarily pro-American or pro-British. In fact, many of them were pro-**Islamic**, and like many **Muslims** throughout the world, most Iraqi Muslims felt that the Western powers were essentially anti-Islamic. Even after Saddam himself was captured on 13 December 2003, resistance to the occupation continued, and attacks on US forces continued – almost daily. Many Iraqi civilians were killed or injured in these attacks as well.

Plans to hand power back to the Iraqis also progressed slowly. The Bush administration announced plans to hand power over to the Iraqi Governing Council in June 2004, although **coalition** troops would remain beyond that time. However, many Iraqis

On 22 April 2003 Iraqi Shi'as march around a holy site in Karbala to mark one of their most important religious anniversaries. Under Saddam such gatherings had been forbidden.

distrusted the Governing Council because its members had been appointed by the US, and believed that elections were necessary before the transfer of power. On 8 March 2004, the Iraqi Governing Council signed an interim **constitution**. This document laid out the plans for Iraq after the occupying forces hand power back to the Iraqis in June 2004.

The new Iraq faces many challenges. One of the most important will be developing a system of government that Iraq's three main groups – the **Sunni Kurds** of the north, the Sunni Arabs of the centre and the **Shi'a** Arabs of the south – will find acceptable. Saddam and his torturers are gone, and many educated **exiles** are returning. With good government and international help, there is a good chance that Iraq's oil wealth can now be used to rebuild and develop the country. Elections for a new national assembly are planned for early 2005, but it is too soon to tell whether true democracy will take hold in Iraq.

Appendix
Chronology of Events

1918 Britain takes control of Iraq from defeated Turks

1927 Britain recognizes Iraq's independence

1937 Saddam Hussein born in Tikrit

1948 First Arab-Israeli War

1958 *July* Free Officers overthrow the monarchy in Iraq; Kassem becomes military dictator

1959 *October* Saddam Hussein takes part in Ba'athist attempt to assassinate Kassem

1963 *February* Kassem overthrown

1967 Second Arab-Israeli War

1968 *July* Aref overthrown by Ba'ath coup, led by al-Bakr. Saddam his right-hand man.

1969 *January* Saddam appointed vice-president

1972 Nationalization of the Iraqi Petroleum Company

1973 Third Arab-Israeli War leads to Arab oil **embargo** and oil price rises

1975 Iraq accepts midstream border in the Shatt al-Arab in exchange for Iran stopping its support of the **Kurds**.

1978 Saddam expels Ayatollah Khomeini from Iraq

1979 *January* Iranian Revolution brings Ayatollah Khomeini to power. *July* Al-Bakr resigns and Saddam becomes president.

1980 *September* Iraq attacks Iran, captures city of Khorramshahr

1981 Israeli bombers destroy Iraq's only nuclear reactor

1982 *May* Iranians recapture Khorramshahr

1984–8 'Tanker War' and 'War of the Cities'

1987 *July* **UN** Resolution 598 calls for a **ceasefire**. Iraq refuses.

1988 *March* Iraqi gas attack on Halabja.

July Iran accepts Resolution 598.

1990 *July* Saddam's meeting with US Ambassador Glaspie.
August Iraq invades Kuwait; UN Resolution 660 condemns Iraq.
November UN Resolution 678 allows the use of 'any means necessary' to free Kuwait.

1991 *January* 'Desert Storm' air war against Iraq begins.
February Ground war begins; ceasefire called.
March **Shi'a** and Kurd uprisings.

1991–8 **UNSCOM** weapon inspectors in Iraq

1995 Defection of Saddam's sons-in-law

1996 UN Resolution 986 allows Iraq to sell oil to buy food and medicines

1998 *December* UNSCOM withdraws from Iraq; 'Desert Fox' bombing attacks

2001 *September* **Terrorist** attacks in New York City and Washington, DC. 'War on Terrorism' declared. Taliban regime overthrown in Afghanistan.

2002 *January* George W. Bush's 'axis of evil' speech. The USA demands 'regime-change' in Iraq.
September Iraq invites weapon inspectors to return.
November UN Resolution 1441 sets conditions for return of weapons inspectors to Iraq.

2003 *February* The USA and Britain call for second UN resolution to act as trigger for war.
March USA and Britain invade Iraq.
April Collapse of Saddam Hussein's regime.
December Saddam captured near Tikrit.

2004 Attacks on civilians and **coalition** forces continue.
March Interim **constitution** signed.

Further Reading

Aburish, Saïd K., *Saddam Hussein: The Politics of Revenge* (Bloomsbury, 2000)

Cockburn, Andrew and Patrick, *Saddam Hussein* (Verso books, 2002)

Mackey, Sandra, *The Reckoning: Iraq and the Legacy of Saddam Hussein* (W. W. Norton, 2002)

Sluglett, Peter and Marion (ed.), *The Times Guide to the Middle East* (Times Books, 1996)

Tripp, Charles, *A History of Iraq* (Cambridge University Press, 2002)

A useful guide to this and other recent international conflicts is Patrick Brogan's *World Conflicts* (Bloomsbury, 1998)

Useful Websites

http://news.bbc.co.uk/1/hi/world/middle_east
BBC Middle East news

www.amnesty.org
Amnesty International

www.cbc.ca/news/indepth/iraq
CBC

www.cnn.com/World
CNN

www.guardian.co.uk/iraq
The *Guardian*

www.observer.co.uk/iraq
The *Observer*

Glossary

abstain decline to vote either for or against

annex add, take over

Arab nationalism idea that Arab interests can best be promoted through Arab unity

attrition wearing down slowly

autonomy some degree of self-government, but not full independence

Ba'ath set of ideas stressing Arab unity and modernization which led to the creation of political parties in several countries, e.g. Syria and Iraq

biological weapons weapons employing viruses/bacteria found in nature

ceasefire agreed end to a period of fighting

censorship limiting of free expression in newspapers, books, films etc.

Central Intelligence Agency (CIA) US federal bureau responsible for intelligence and counter-intelligence activities outside the USA

chemical weapons weapons employing synthetic poisons

civil war war between different groups in one country

coalition temporary alliance, often of political parties in government or nations with a common goal

Cold War not a real war, but political hostility between Western countries and the Soviet bloc (1945–90)

colonialism rule of underdeveloped countries by advanced countries, economically speaking

communist believer in communism, a political theory and practice which puts the interests of society as a whole above the interests of individuals

Congress law-making arm of the US government, comprising the Senate and House of Representatives

constitution in politics, the way a country is set up to safeguard its fundamental principles

conventional weapons weapons such as guns, tanks and planes

coup violent seizure of power

democracy political system in which governments are regularly elected by the mass of the people (or a country in which this system exists)

deployment moving troops into position ready for action

elite group of people thought to be the best

embargo refusal to trade

exile barred from one's own country

Geneva Convention series of international agreements on how wars should be fought. The first was agreed in 1864; there have been others in 1907, 1929, 1949 and 1977.

hostage person seized with the intention of forcing others to act in a certain way

human rights basic rights which should belong to any person

infrastructure economic foundations of a society

intelligence information gathered of military or political use

Islam one of world's three major monotheistic (one God) religions (along with Christianity and Judaism), founded by the Prophet Muhammad in the 7th century

Islamic republic government which bases its laws on the laws of Islam

Kurds Middle Eastern people, mostly Sunni Muslims, who have no state of their own but form large minorities in Turkey, Iran and Iraq

military dictatorship government by unelected members of the armed forces

monarchy state which has supreme ruler, such as a king, at its head

monitoring device type of equipment which keeps a continuous watch

Muslim follower of Islam

nationalize take into government ownership

non-conventional weapons nuclear, biological or chemical weapons

OPEC Organization of Petroleum Exporting Countries, which includes most of the major oil producers, and which agrees how much oil each will produce in any given period

Palestine Liberation Organization (PLO) party which wants to unite Palestinian Arab groups

penicillin essential drug for fighting many types of disease

political police police concerned with preventing political opposition to the regime in power

reparation payment to make amends for war damage

republic state where people have elected the president

sanctions economic measures, such as stoppage of trade, to persuade a country to change its policies

secular unconcerned with religion or religious identities

Shi'a Muslims smaller of two major Muslim groups

smart bomb bomb which is guided to its target, usually by laser or radio

Stalinist like the Soviet ruler Stalin, who allowed no opposition whatsoever

stereotype typical example, often exaggerated

Sunni Muslims larger of two major Muslim groups

terrorism use of violence and intimidation against ordinary people for political ends

treason betrayal of one's own country

United Nations (UN) association of countries formed in 1945 to promote world peace

United Nations Security Council council within the UN most responsible for the maintenance of world peace and security. It has five permanent members – the USA, Russia, Britain, France and China – and ten rotating members chosen from other member states.

UNSCOM United National Special Commission, set up in 1991 to carry out weapons inspection in Iraq

veto reject, block (usually a resolution or a bill)

weapons of mass destruction weapons capable of killing thousands, or laying waste large areas, at a single blow. They are usually subdivided into nuclear, chemical and biological weapons.

welfare state state that makes itself responsible for all its citizens, particularly those without jobs, in ill health, and beyond working age

Index